SHORT WALKS YORKSHIRE DALES

GRASSINGTON, SKIPTON, MALHAM AND ILKLEY

Rachel Crolla and Carl McKeating

On the walled path to Linton Falls (Walk 10)

CONTENTS

Using this guide.. 4
Route summary table 6
Map key... 7
Introduction.. 9
   Walking in the Yorkshire Dales.. 10
   Things to see 10
   Bases and places to stay... 11
   Travel 11

The Walks

1.	Ilkley Moor, White Wells and the Cow and Calf rocks..............	13
2.	Heber's Ghyll and the Swastika Stone	19
3.	Bolton Abbey and the Strid...	25
4.	Simon's Seat and the Valley of Desolation......................	31
5.	Burnsall, Appletreewick and Kail Hill	35
6.	Burnsall and Hebden by way of the Wharfe...................	39
7.	Trollers Gill	45
8.	Grimwith Reservoir...	49
9.	Grassington lead mines from Hebden	55
10.	Grassington, Linton Falls and Linton	61
11.	Grassington Grass Wood and Ghaistrill's Strid................	67
12.	Conistone Dib and Pie	73
13.	Malham Cove, Gordale Scar and Janet's Foss.................	79
14.	Embsay Crag and Reservoir	85
15.	Skipton Woods and Castle	89

Useful information... 95

USING THIS GUIDE

Routes in this book

In this book you will find a selection of easy or moderate walks suitable for almost everyone, including casual walkers and families with children, or for when you only have a short time to fill. The routes have been carefully chosen to allow you to explore the area and its attractions. Most routes are circular or out-and-back, although some linear walks may be included that use public transport to get back to the start. Although there may be some climbs there is no challenging terrain, but do bear in mind that conditions can sometimes be wet or muddy underfoot. A route summary table is included on page 6 to help you choose the right walk.

Clothing and footwear

You won't need any special equipment to enjoy these walks. The weather in Britain can be changeable, so choose clothing suitable for the season and wear or carry a waterproof jacket. For footwear, comfortable walking boots or trainers with a good grip are best. A small rucksack for drinks, snacks and spare clothing is useful. See www.adventuresmart.uk.

Walk descriptions

At the beginning of each walk you'll find all the information you need:

- start/finish location, with a what3words address to help you find it
- parking and transport information, estimated walking time, total distance and climb
- details of public toilets available along the route and where you can get refreshments
- a summary of the key highlights of the walk and what you might see

Timings given are the time to complete the walk at a reasonable walking pace. Allow extra time for extended stops or if walking with children.

The route is described in clear, easy-to-follow directions, with each waypoint marked on an accompanying map extract. It's a good idea to read the whole of the route instructions before setting out, so that you know what to expect.

Maps, GPX files and what3words

Extracts from the OS® 1:25,000 map accompany each route. GPX files for all the walks in this book are available to download at www.cicerone.co.uk/1232/gpx.

What3words is a free smartphone app which identifies every 3m square of the globe with a unique three-word address, e.g. ///destiny.cafe.sonic. For more information see https://what3words.com/products/what3words-app.

USING THIS GUIDE

Walking with children

Even young children can be surprisingly strong walkers, but every family is different and you may need to adapt the timings given in this book to take that into account. Make sure you go at the pace of the slowest member and choose a walk with an exciting objective in mind, such as a cave, river, waterfall or picnic spot. Many of the walks can be shortened to suit – suggestions are included at the end of the route description.

Dogs

Sheep or cattle may be found grazing on a number of these walks. Keep dogs under control at all times so that they don't scare or disturb livestock or wildlife. Cattle, particularly cows with calves, may very occasionally pose a risk to walkers with dogs. If you ever feel threatened by cattle, you should let go of your dog's lead and let it run free.

Enjoying the countryside responsibly

Enjoy the countryside and treat it with respect to protect our natural environments. Stick to footpaths and take your litter home with you. When driving, slow down on rural roads and park considerately, or better still use public transport. For more details check out www.gov.uk/countryside-code.

The Countryside Code

Respect everyone
- be considerate to those living in, working in and enjoying the countryside
- leave gates and property as you find them
- do not block access to gateways or driveways when parking
- be nice, say hello, share the space
- follow local signs and keep to marked paths unless wider access is available

Protect the environment
- take your litter home – leave no trace of your visit
- do not light fires and only have BBQs where signs say you can
- always keep dogs under control and in sight
- dog poo – bag it and bin it – any public waste bin will do
- care for nature – do not cause damage or disturbance

Enjoy the outdoors
- check your route and local conditions
- plan your adventure – know what to expect and what you can do
- enjoy your visit, have fun, make a memory

SHORT WALKS YORKSHIRE DALES

ROUTE SUMMARY TABLE

WALK NAME	START POINT	TIME	DISTANCE
1. Ilkley Moor, White Wells and the Cow and Calf rocks	Ilkley train station	2hr	5.5km (3½ miles)
2. Heber's Ghyll and the Swastika Stone	Ilkley train station	2hr	6.5km (4 miles)
3. Bolton Abbey and the Strid	Bolton Abbey	2½hr	10km (6¼ miles)
4. Simon's Seat and the Valley of Desolation (Challenge)	Bolton Abbey	3½–4hr	10.5km (6½ miles)
5. Burnsall, Appletreewick and Kail Hill	Burnsall Bridge	2hr	6.5km (4 miles)
6. Burnsall and Hebden by way of the Wharfe	Burnsall Bridge	1½hr	6km (3½ miles)
7. Trollers Gill	Parcevall Hall Gardens, Skyreholme	1½hr	3.5km (2¼ miles)
8. Grimwith Reservoir	Grimwith Reservoir car park	2hr	7km (4¼ miles)
9. Grassington lead mines from Hebden	Hebden village centre	2½hr	8km (5 miles)
10. Grassington, Linton Falls and Linton	Grassington market square	2hr	6km (3¾ miles)
11. Grassington Grass Wood and Ghaistrill's Strid	Grassington market square	2½hr	7km (4¼ miles)
12. Conistone Dib and Pie	Conistone Bridge	1½hr	4.5km (2¾ miles)
13. Malham Cove, Gordale Scar and Janet's Foss	Malham village centre	2½hr	8km (5 miles)
14. Embsay Crag and Reservoir	Embsay village centre	2hr	5.5km (3½ miles)
15. Skipton Woods and Castle	Skipton Castle	1½hr	3.5km (2¼ miles)

ROUTE SUMMARY TABLE

HIGHLIGHTS
Historic spa town and plunge pool, iconic rocks
Secluded wooded gill, famous moor and ancient stones
Splendid abbey and riverside trails
Superb views, rocky summit and waterfalls
Two pretty Dales villages and Wharfedale views
Charming villages and riverside picnic spots
Scenic rocky gorge and old mines
Nature spotting at a high and tranquil reservoir
Fascinating old mineworks, waterfalls
Pretty villages and riverside scenery
Charming woodland and river rapids
Limestone gorge and fell-top rock formations
Must-see natural wonder, limestone paving and falls
Low fell with great views across the water
Popular market town, medieval castle, ancient woodland

SYMBOLS USED ON ROUTE MAPS

 Start point

 Finish point

 Start and finish at the same place

 Waypoint

~ Route line

MAPPING IS SHOWN AT A SCALE OF 1:25,000

0 KM 0.25 0.5
0 miles 0.25

DOWNLOAD THE GPX FILES FOR FREE AT
www.cicerone.co.uk/1232/gpx

The Cow and Calf rocks stand guard over Ilkley (Walk 1)

INTRODUCTION

The vast expanse of limestone at Malham Cove (Walk 13)

Dry stone walls, grazing sheep, heather-clad fell tops, tea-box villages and curious rock formations wherever you go – the Yorkshire Dales has its own distinct charm and the southern part of the national park covered by this guidebook is no exception. The walks in this book combine the best of the two most accessible dales: Wharfedale, which snakes north from the stately spa town of Ilkley towards Grassington;, and Airedale, north of the traditional 'Gateway to the Dales' market town of Skipton. An array of spectacular sites awaits, including Bolton Abbey, Malham Cove, Gordale Scar, Janet's Foss, Linton Falls, Simon's Seat, the Strid, Cow and Calf rocks, Kilnsey Crag and Trollers Gill.

The valleys or 'dales' were formed in the Ice Age, when glacial waters began to carve out the landscape. The eye-catching rock features in the area are even older – it is difficult to believe that some of the hill or 'fell' tops were once reefs in tropical seas; the limestone of Malham and Conistone contains fossils of ancient seashells. Above the rivers and sheep-grazing fields, it is easy to reach open moorland where kites and curlews circle overhead. Here you will find rough gritstone rocks such as the Cow and Calf – which command the view over Ilkley

– and Simon's Seat, the most prominent fell overlooking Wharfedale. Elsewhere the vestiges of former farming practices can be seen in the field barns or 'laithes' in the valleys, while the lead mining heritage of the dales can be discovered near Grassington and at Trollers Gill.

Walking in the Yorkshire Dales

This area is blessed with numerous good paths and rights of way, particularly along scenic sections of riverbank. Many of the routes link some of the loveliest Dales villages, most of which are served by excellent tea rooms and pubs. As well as incorporating the best sites of the area, some of the walks can be combined with visits to places of interest such as Skipton Castle or Parcevall Hall Gardens.

The southern Yorkshire Dales are hilly, but not mountainous. A few walks include ascents of small fells, but these are not long or arduous and should be well within the capabilities of the average person. Expect mainly good paths and tracks in the valleys, sometimes with stone stiles in fields still used for sheep and occasionally cattle farming. The walks also include woodland and moorland, though nowhere should ever get excessively muddy.

All the routes in the book should be easy to follow and signposting is generally good throughout the national park, especially on the popular long-distance Dales Way. Route-finding can become a little more challenging on Ilkley Moor, where a veritable maze of paths exists. When crossing through Dales fields, a good strategy is to look ahead to spot the next stone stile and make a beeline for it. Stiles in the drystone walls (usually stone steps or 'squeeze' types) are a feature of Dales walking and should not pose any difficulty to most people (although dogs may need a hand).

Things to see

Take time to enjoy the waters of the River Wharfe, which has a variety of superb bathing, paddling and picnicking spots. At quieter times, look out for kingfishers and herons here. Malham Cove – frequented by Harry Potter and countless geography field-trippers – is a five-star natural wonder best enjoyed outside of summer weekends and bank holidays. Explore Coniston Dib and Trollers Gill for more solitary limestone experiences. Bolton Priory is another quintessential Dales site – early mornings or evenings are best to appreciate its beauty and spot deer in the woodland. The walks can be appreciated out of season: take a New Year's dip in Ilkley's White Wells plunge pool or visit a frosty Simon's Seat, when the Valley of Desolation loses its verdant clothing and earns its name.

Bolton Priory stands guard over the River Wharfe (Walk 3)

For plover, widgeon and Canada geese, the isolated Grimwith Reservoir is hard to beat, whereas you would be unlucky not to see curlew and red kites on the moorland walks. Late summer is the time to see the swathes of purple heather adorning the hillsides.

Bases and places to stay

Grassington, Ilkley and Skipton all have plenty of accommodation options and are convenient for public transport, shops and places to eat. The smaller villages such as Appletreewick, Burnsall and Malham are also good choices. There are numerous campsites and B&Bs and the area is compact enough that all the walks can be visited from any of these bases.

Travel

Ilkley and Skipton are well served by rail. The excellent and economical DalesBus service means that all the walks in this book can be accessed by public transport. Grassington and Malham are served by regular buses, whereas for Burnsall, Hebden and Appletreewick, services are more limited and you should plan ahead accordingly. Drivers should expect narrow roads with passing places, frequently used by farm vehicles.

Legend says the Calf rock was thrown here by the giant Rombald

WALK 1
Ilkley Moor, White Wells and the Cow and Calf rocks

Time 2hr
Distance 5.5km (3½ miles)
Climb 260m

Walk up from the spa town onto Ilkley's famous moor, passing landmark rocks, and visiting the historic plunge pool at White Wells

Start/finish	Ilkley train station
Locate	///tiny.revives.plump
Cafes/pubs	Great choice in Ilkley, seasonal cafes at White Wells and Cow and Calf car park
Transport	Trains from Leeds and Bradford every half hour
Parking	Free parking at Darwin Gardens or White Wells car parks on Wells Road (LS29 9TF)
Toilets	At White Wells, Cow and Calf parking, Ilkley town car park

A panoramic walk from the well-heeled town of Ilkley, up onto its famous moor – immortalised in the famous Baht' at song. The walk passes White Wells – a vestige of Ilkley's past as a spa for people to take the restorative waters. Views from the moor give way to the town's landmark Cow and Calf rocks, which have drawn tourists for over 200 years. A visit to the lovely Ilkley Tarn on the return completes this satisfying circuit.

Generations of rock chisellers have left their mark at the Cow and Calf

1 Use the zebra crossing then go right then left to walk up Wells Road until you reach Darwin Gardens. There is a free car park here. Continue up Wells Road for 200m, passing Wells House to reach the White Wells car park. The biologist Charles Darwin came to White Wells in 1859 to take the curative waters of Ilkley.

2 Turn left at the car park and follow a good track up to the visible **White**

The crags of Rocky Valley

Wells building. There is a seasonal cafe (open when a flag is flying) at the bath house here. Visitors can take the plunge in the supposedly healing waters of the spring inside the building.

3 The track continues up the right side of the building (facing it) along the Millennium Way. The crags of **Rocky Valley** are soon seen up ahead; the track leads up stone steps to the right of these. At the top continue straight ahead on the main path for around 200m to a clear crossroads of paths.

4 Turn left and after a further 200m, the tops of the Cow and Calf rocks are visible below. Stay on the main path which now descends to the popular picnic area of **Backstone Beck**. Cross this on the left-hand route on flat slabs and continue, to emerge at the steep-sided quarry edge of the **Cow and Calf** area. Take time to visit the top of the Cow rock just to the left. The rocks are adorned with Victorian carvings and often more modern additions.

5 Retrace your steps around the edge of the quarry, where a clear path

> ⓘ *From Ilkley Moor there are great views of the town and its eye-catching lido. The outdoor swimming pool opened in 1935 as part of the Silver Jubilee celebrations of George V.*

Flat slabs at Backstone Beck high above Ilkley with Beamsley Beacon beyond

> ⓘ **Ilkley Moor is festooned with countless meandering paths. Should you take a wrong turn, rest assured that heading downhill will bring you back to civilisation and the town centre.**

leads down to the cafe, toilets and car park. Visit the nearby Calf rock then go back to the car park and take care to find a gravel path signed to Ilkley. This does not lead to the Calf but traverses beneath it, to arrive at a path junction after 400m.

6 Head uphill on the left-hand option signed to Backstone Beck and the tarn. After 100m the path arrives at a footbridge over Backstone Beck. Just before the bridge you can make a short detour for 30m along a path uphill to the left to visit the Beck Stone.

The Beck Stone is one of six Stanza poetry stones located on the Yorkshire moors. It has a poem by poet laureate Simon Armitage chiselled into it, but it can be hard to locate in summer when the bracken is high.

7 Cross the footbridge and continue for around 300m to reach a lovely man-made tarn. Go round the

WALK 1 – ILKLEY MOOR, WHITE WELLS AND THE COW AND CALF ROCKS

tarn on either side and pick up a tarmac path at its end and follow this to a gate; here turn left past a 1920s paddling pool to regain Wells Road. Retrace your outbound route to your start point.

> **− To shorten**
> Starting from White Wells car park saves around 20min and is 1km shorter.
>
> **+ To lengthen**
> At the crossroads of paths above Rocky Valley, staying straight on leads to the Neolithic Twelve Apostles stone circle. Retrace your steps to join the main route. This adds 2.5km and at least 30min.

Legends of Ilkley

Ilkley Moor is a weird and wonderful place. According to one legend, the smaller Calf rock was split from the Cow by the giant Rombald, who was fleeing his angry wife. Another legend tells of a shepherd who injured his leg on the moor and healed it by bathing in the waters at White Wells. The spa plunge pool was built in 1700. Other strange tales of the moor include sightings of pixies, ghosts and even aliens.

On the top of the Cow rock on Ilkley Moor

The enchanting woods of Heber's Ghyll

WALK 2
Heber's Ghyll and the Swastika Stone

Time 2hr
Distance 6.5km (4 miles)
Climb 220m

Hidden waterfalls, ancient carvings and stately mansions on the edge of Ilkley Moor

Start/finish	Ilkley train station
Locate	///tiny.revives.plump
Cafes/pubs	Great choice in Ilkley
Transport	Trains from Leeds and Bradford every half hour
Parking	Considerate on-street parking on Queen's Drive and free car park at Darwin Gardens (LS29 9TF)
Toilets	Town centre car park (100m off route)

A large part of Ilkley's appeal is its superb setting at the foot of sweeping moorland. This walk ascends wooded footpaths right from the town centre, through Ilkley's most well-heeled quarters, to reach Heber's Ghyll – a woodland watercourse reminiscent of the land that time forgot. The walk's second half visits the mysterious ancient Swastika Stone and follows the edge of the panoramic moor back into town.

Looking out across Wharfedale from the Swastika Stone

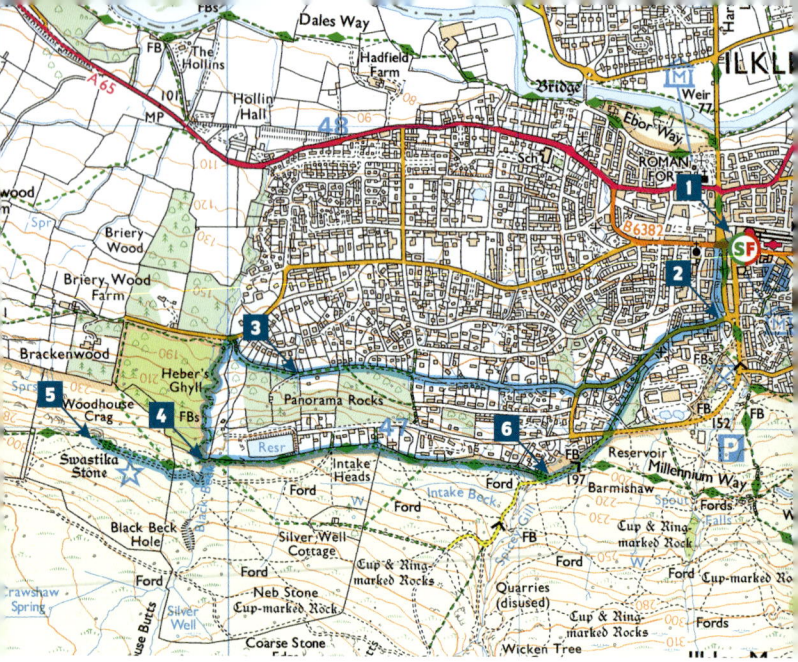

1 Cross the zebra crossing outside the station. Turn right for 30m to an area with benches at the bottom of Wells Promenade and a large sign for Mill Ghyll. Follow the main footpath under a small footbridge up the watercourse to the top of Mill Ghyll. Mill Ghyll feels remarkably peaceful and secluded despite its proximity to Ilkley's main shopping street.

2 Emerging from the ghyll, take Queen's Road right, touring some exclusive and historic town dwellings – blue plaques abound here. Pass St Margaret's Church and 200m beyond this, go right off Queen's Road onto the dead-end Queen's Drive. Follow this to its end where it becomes a track, then tarmac again and finally a private road with a footpath beside it. For those with cars, the walk can be shortened by parking considerately in this area.

> ⓘ *If you see smoke in the distance across the valley, the most common reason is managed fires on grouse moors. New and tasty young shoots of heather are encouraged by burning older plants.*

The stately spa town of Ilkley from the moor

3 Continue on the main path, veering right and downhill for a short time until steps emerge at a small road bridge with a sign for **Heber's Ghyll**. Don't cross the road or bridge, but turn back uphill along a delightful wooded path beside the stream, crossing several footbridges as you climb onto the moor.

4 Head left at the top of the ghyll, crossing a final footbridge at the edge of the moor to reach a more open area with benches and small gritstone outcrops. Instead of taking the main path, turn right on a smaller path uphill, still following the line of the stream. This path meets a large gravel track after 100m. Turn right along the track. From a gate after 50m head towards the metal railings surrounding the **Swastika Stone**.

5 After visiting the stone, follow the track and path back to the bench area near the top of Heber's Ghyll. Take the good path rightwards along the edge of the moor. Pass a small **reservoir** and continue for 1km. There are views of Rocky Valley (Walk 1) ahead.

6 The path eventually emerges at a dead-end road; turn left on this downhill. At a T-junction, go straight ahead

Skirting the edge of the moor with Rocky Valley beyond

on another wooded path downhill. This path leads to St Margaret's Church. Retrace your outbound route to the town centre and the station.

Alternatively, keep heading straight down more footpaths to return to The Grove shopping street.

The ancient markings of the mystical Swastika Stone

WALK 2 – HEBER'S GHYLL AND THE SWASTIKA STONE

− To shorten

Park on Queen's Drive to start the walk before Waypoint 3. At Waypoint 6, walk down the road then turn left at the T-junction; this becomes Queen's Road. Head downhill and then turn left on Queen's Drive. This is 30min shorter.

+ To lengthen

Combine with Walk 1 for a 12km walk taking 4hr. At Waypoint 6 instead of descending the road back into Ilkley, cross over and continue along the same path which will lead to the White Wells track on Walk 1.

The Swastika Stone and ancient carvings of Ilkley Moor

The Swastika Stone probably dates back to the Bronze Age or early Iron Age when, in many ancient civilisations, this curly swastika symbol represented the sun. Evidence of early dwellers is scattered throughout the moor; those who are interested can follow paths to visit more than two dozen carved rocks in the area and see numerous cup and ring markings.

Many theories have been proposed about this early rock art: maps, shamanic sacrifice sites, boundary stones or grave markers. Whatever the original purpose, the stones add to the mystical quality of the moor.

On Ilkley Moor baht 'at

The superb ruins of Bolton Priory

WALK 3
Bolton Abbey and the Strid

Start/finish	Bolton Abbey village centre
Locate	///lease.speeded.fellow
Cafes/pubs	In Bolton Abbey village, Cavendish Pavilion and Strid car park
Transport	DalesBus from Ilkley
Parking	Bolton Abbey car park (BD23 6EX)
Toilets	In car park and at Cavendish Pavilion

Time 2½hr
Distance 10km (6¼ miles)
Climb 220m

A striking riverside priory and the River Wharfe at its most tranquil and most tumultuous

The quintessential Wharfedale walk; Bolton Priory and ruins inhabit a magnificent spot on a sweeping bend of the River Wharfe. Here the river is peaceful and there are good beaches; further upstream the river forms the ferocious chasm of the Strid – a place steeped in a macabre history. Good paths on both riverbanks make a great circular outing in either direction. This is a popular walk, so a visit is best outside peak times.

Bolton Priory's impressive ruins

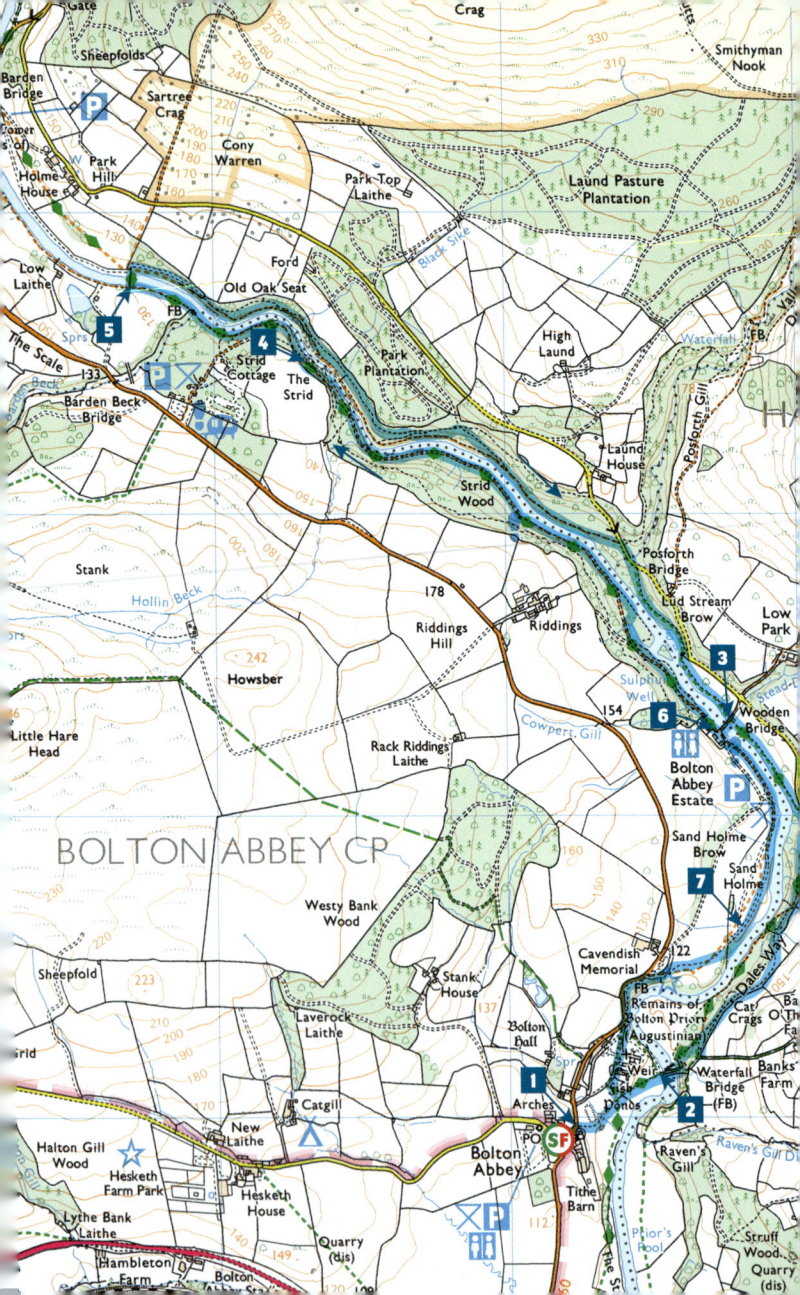

1 From the village centre, take a path through an opening in an ancient stone wall near the antique book shop. Go down to the obvious **priory church and ruins**. The priory ruins and church are free to explore.

2 After visiting the ruins, cross the footbridge or use the stepping stones in low water conditions. Turn left uphill on the gravel path skirting the hillside above the river then descending to join a minor road at a ford. Cross a footbridge here and immediately leave the road on a path in the same direction to reach a large **wooden bridge** on the left at the Cavendish Pavilion.

3 Cross the bridge and turn right, taking the path heading up the opposite side of the river through pleasant woodland. The path forks twice: both times take the lower and wider path straight on through **Strid Wood** beside the flat and calm river. After 1km the river changes character, its bed becoming rockier as it reaches **the Strid**.

The treacherous and gloomy waters of the Strid

> The Strid – so named as it is a tempting-looking narrow stride across – is well signed with boards alerting visitors to the hidden hazards of the waters. After winter rain, the river pounds through the narrow chasm and the dangers become obvious. Even on the brightest summer's day, the Strid is a rather gloomy and moss-ridden place.

4 After observing the Strid from a safe distance, follow the same path upstream, initially steeply. Ignore any forks left to the Strid Wood car park. Join a wide gravel path and take the lower option towards Barden Bridge at the next junction. The path emerges from the wood on a grassy stretch to reach a turreted bridge. This bridge is a former aqueduct that delivered

Returning to Bolton Abbey from the Cavendish Pavilion

water from the Nidderdale reservoirs to nearby towns.

5 Cross the bridge and turn right to return along the opposite riverbank. Go through meadows and then gain height on a narrower path traversing the steep-sided banks of the river. There are good views back to the Strid from here. After 600m the path descends and winds beside the riverbank passing some islands to reach the bridge at the Cavendish Pavilion again.

6 Recross the river and turn left on a track through the car park, staying close to the river.

7 Take the path leading out the opposite end of the car park through a gate. More dramatic views of the priory ruins unfold. Swing rightwards uphill to reach the road at the **Cavendish Memorial** fountain. Turn left on the roadside path for 100m, then go through a gate into the abbey estate to the front of the priory church. From here, rejoin the outbound route back to the village centre.

> ⓘ *The Bolton Abbey estate includes nearly 30,000 acres of land on both the east and west sides of the River Wharfe and huge swathes of Barden Moor. It is owned by the Duke and Duchess of Devonshire, who also own the Chatsworth Estate in Derbyshire.*

WALK 3 – BOLTON ABBEY AND THE STRID

− To shorten

Cut the loop short by crossing the bridge at the Cavendish Pavilion at Waypoint 3, giving a walk of just under 4km (1hr).

+ To lengthen

For a longer walk of 11.5km (3hr), at Waypoint 5 continue along the riverside path to Barden Bridge. The 15th-century ruins of Barden Tower can be visited by turning left for 100m up the road. Cross Barden Bridge to return to the main route on the opposite bank of the river.

Bolton Abbey and the Strid

The Bolton Abbey estate is owned by the Duke and Duchess of Devonshire – the Cavendish family. Augustinian canons lived in Bolton Priory from the 12th century until the dissolution of the monasteries. The priory church is still used today and contains a small exhibition about the history of the location. The Strid has gained notoriety for a series of drownings, including a tragic honeymooning couple in the 1990s.

A heritage steam railway runs for 6.5km between the village of Bolton Abbey and Embsay (Walk 14) on the former Skipton to Ilkley rail line. Visitors can make the journey in restored Victorian and Edwardian carriages.

Crossing the stepping stones at Bolton Priory

The hidden falls in the Valley of Desolation

WALK 4
Simon's Seat and the Valley of Desolation

CHALLENGE ROUTE

Time 3½– 4hr
Distance 10.5km (6½ miles)
Climb 450m

Climb to the rocky fell top of the best summit in Lower Wharfedale via a verdant valley and waterfall

Start/finish	*Cavendish Pavilion, Bolton Abbey*
Locate	*///segregate.glove.triangles*
Cafes/pubs	*Cafe at start of route*
Transport	*DalesBus from Ilkley*
Parking	*Paid Riverside car park (BD23 6HU)*
Toilets	*At Cavendish Pavilion*

Simon's Seat is the crowning glory of lower Wharfedale: its craggy 485m high summit catches the eye from many of the walks in this book. There is no better seat on which to enjoy a sandwich and superb views. This walk through the Bolton Abbey estate to the beautiful moorland summit more than repays the effort of the lengthier outing, a section of rockier paths, and the longer – although generally gradual – ascent. The route, which goes over access land, may occasionally be closed to the public during grouse shooting season, and dogs are not permitted.

The moorland track descending Simon's Seat

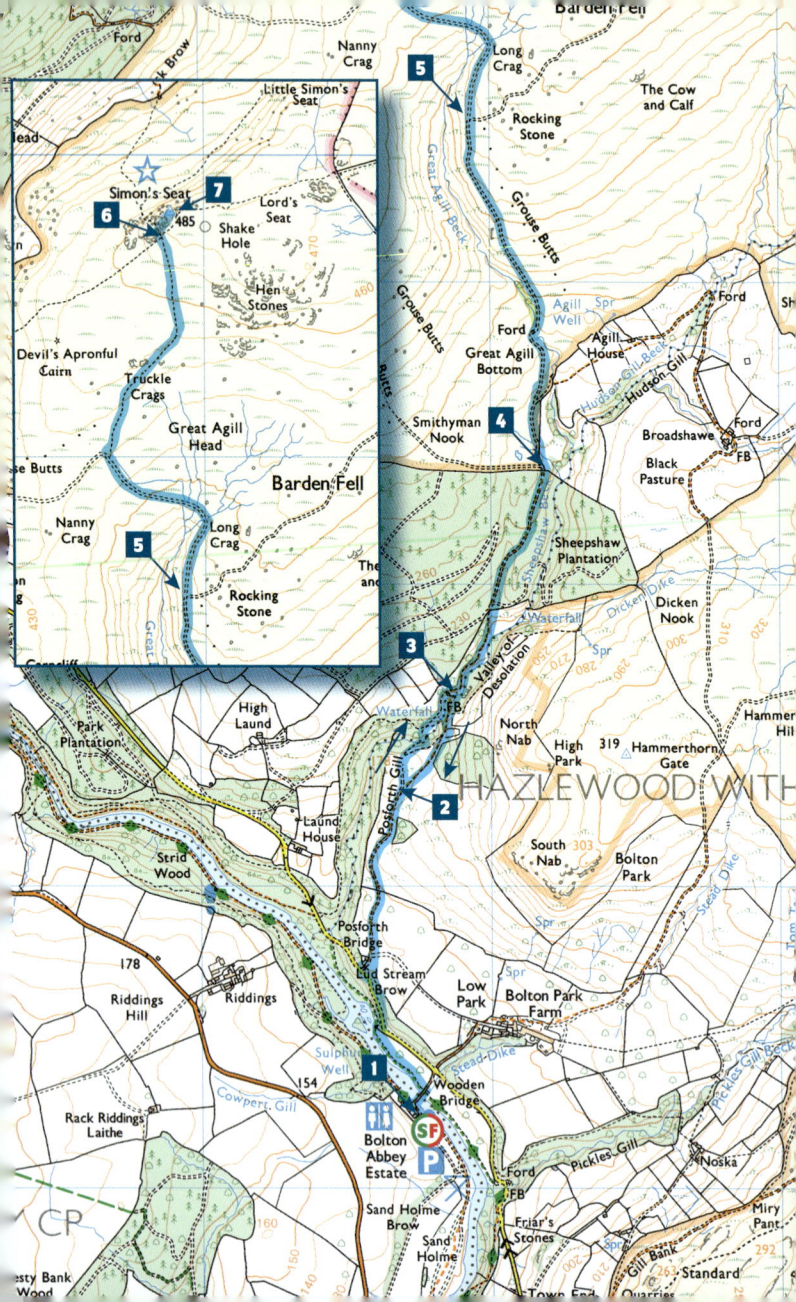

WALK 4 – SIMON'S SEAT AND THE VALLEY OF DESOLATION

1 Cross the wooden footbridge by the Cavendish Pavilion and take the path left beside the river initially. At a gate, head sharply right signed to Simon's Seat. This path climbs to a minor road. Turn left along it for 70m, then take a signed path right towards the Valley of Desolation. Follow the wide track, passing some enormous oak trees and a small reedy pond after 500m.

2 Shortly after the pond there is a bench at the top of a small rise with a view of a surprising waterfall. Head down the narrow path here into the **Valley of Desolation**, crossing a footbridge and going up the left side of the beck to view the falls at closer quarters. Continue on the path up the left side of the falls to reach a wooden footbridge.

The Valley of Desolation now seems misnamed; it is actually a lush and verdant place. The curious name was given after a storm in 1836 wreaked havoc in the gill and across Barden Moor.

3 Do not cross the footbridge, but follow the left side of **Posforth Gill Beck** uphill on a narrow path, until a gate brings you out to join a track and more open land. This section of trickier terrain does not last long. Continue on the track to another gate.

4 Head straight on at the gate, now on a well-made track winding up beside **Great Agill Beck** for 1km through bracken and heather-covered slopes. This never becomes too steep.

5 At a stone picnic table, the rocky head of Simon's Seat shows itself on the horizon. Stay straight on at a first track junction towards the rock outcrops, skirting across the top of Great Agill Beck at Great Agill Head. Bear

Truckle Crags on route to Simon's Seat

right at a second split, still heading towards the crags. Pass to the right of **Truckle Crags** – a first outcrop of rock – before reaching the obvious towers of **Simon's Seat**.

> No-one is quite sure who Simon was – the most interesting possibility is that the fell is named after a baby who was found by a shepherd on the craggy summit. Nearby rocky outcrops have the matching but rather grander names of Earl's Seat and Lord's Seat.

6 Look for the easiest ground to the right of the steeper rocks to clamber easily up to the summit and trig point and try to decide exactly where Simon himself might have sat to take in the superb views.

Much of Lower Wharfedale including Grimwith Reservoir (Walk 8), Trollers Gill (Walk 7) and Kail Hill (Walk 5) is on display from Simon's Seat, along with the distinctive white 'golf balls' of RAF Menwith Hill to the east.

7 After exploring the summit rocks, retrace your steps to the footbridge above the waterfall. Cross this and head down the clear path to rejoin the outbound route below the falls and follow this back to the start point.

– To shorten

The walk can be cut short at the waterfalls, which make a worthwhile outing in themselves, giving a walk of 2.5km (45min).

Looking out across Wharfedale from Simon's Seat

WALK 5
Burnsall, Appletreewick and Kail Hill

Time 2hr
Distance 6.5km (4 miles)
Climb 155m

A varied walk exploring the quieter side of Burnsall along the River Wharfe and following walled tracks over a small fell

Start/finish	*Burnsall Bridge*
Locate	*///rivers.hillsides.bleak*
Cafes/pubs	*Cafes and pub in Burnsall, two pubs in Appletreewick and cafe/ice-cream at Masons campsite*
Transport	*DalesBus services from Grassington and Ilkley*
Parking	*Paid car parking (BD23 6BS) and limited on-street parking*
Toilets	*In village car park*

The scenic bending river and arched stone bridge at Burnsall make the village a popular destination for summer walkers and bathers. The beautiful village is cupped by low-lying Dales fells and this route explores one of them, climbing gradually via dry-stone-walled tracks over Kail Hill and affording great views of Wharfedale. Downstream of Burnsall is the tucked-away village of Appletreewick, which is also visited on this walk via the lovely riverside Dales Way path.

Rainbow over the Wharfe and the Dales Way path near Appletreewick

1 Cross Burnsall's five-arched bridge away from the village. Shortly afterwards turn right on a path signed as the Dales Way to Appletreewick and follow this across the field to a bank of trees beside the **River Wharfe**. Follow the river downstream, after 800m crossing a small footbridge over Barben Beck.

2 Directly after the footbridge, turn left – away from the riverside Dales Way which is the return route – up a walled track. This leads gently uphill to a minor road. Cross the road, continuing more definitively uphill on the bridleway straight ahead signed to New Road. This becomes a wonderful drystone-walled track (**Kail Lane**).

WALK 5 – BURNSALL, APPLETREEWICK AND KAIL HILL

Sheep resting in the shade on Kail Hill

Where the path eventually flattens out, there are superb views ahead of Simon's Seat. If you pause to get your breath, look behind you at the curving valley of Wharfedale and its encircling fells.

3 Follow the bridleway around the left side of a farm. After a further 400m, reach a crossroads of paths.

4 Turn right here on a path signed to Appletreewick. Follow the signed path,

On the way up Kail Hill

curving downhill and eventually descending more steeply on a stony track until you emerge beside the Craven Arms pub in **Appletreewick**. The main part of the village is left up the road.

> Appletreewick – sometimes shortened to Ap'trick by locals – has got to be one of the most pleasant-sounding place names in England. The village itself does not disappoint.

5 Turn right at the Craven Arms and walk down the road for 100m. Just before the large campsite, take a path left signed to the riverside. Where the path meets the River Wharfe, turn right and follow the grassy riverbank upstream all the way back to **Burnsall**.

You will rejoin the outbound route about 1km from the end point – retrace your steps back from here.

− To shorten
Just follow the riverside Dales Way footpath to Appletreewick and return the same way, giving a walk of just under 4km (1hr 15min).

✚ To lengthen
Combine this walk with Walk 6, continuing from Burnsall to Hebden for a total distance of just over 12km (3hr 30min).

WALK 6
Burnsall and Hebden by way of the Wharfe

Time 1½hr
Distance 6km (3½ miles)
Climb 120m

A beautiful stroll linking two of the classic Wharfedale villages on riverside paths

Start/finish	Burnsall Bridge
Locate	///rivers.hillsides.bleak
Cafes/pubs	Cafes and pubs in both villages
Transport	DalesBus runs services from Ilkley and Grassington
Parking	Paid and limited on-street parking in Burnsall (BD23 6BS)
Toilets	In Burnsall car park

Burnsall's superb position on a photogenic bend in the River Wharfe ensures the village's popularity. Easy walking upstream alongside the river leads past limestone cliffs over a narrow footbridge to the quieter neighbouring village of Hebden and returns through attractive drystone-walled fields with expansive views. This open stretch of the river, with its pools and rocky banks, is a favourite local bathing spot in summer.

Burnsall's five-arched bridge on the Dales Way path towards Hebden

39

Bathers at Loup Scar near Burnsall

1 Do not cross the bridge out of Burnsall, but take the signed path beside the Red Lion pub. This leads out of the village along the River Wharfe's increasingly open and grassy banks. After 800m the path rises to greet a rockier stretch of shoreline, where the limestone cliffs of **Loup Scar** have provided a jumping challenge for generations of local thrill seekers.

2 Continue for a further 1km to reach a set of **stepping stones** and the safer option of a narrow suspension bridge across the river. Local folklore says that the suspension bridge was built in the 1880s after an unfortunate man called Joseph Slack drowned while crossing the stepping stones.

3 Cross the river and go straight on across a field to reach a minor road.

Crossing the suspension bridge near Hebden

Turn right on this for less than 50m, then take a footpath signed to Hebden between the houses on the left. This path leaves the houses and crosses two small footbridges – the second of which is over Hebden Beck. Follow the beck for 200m, until a short rise brings you out by the playground, tea rooms and church at **Hebden**.

4 Cross directly over the road and walk up Church Lane, with an opportunity to visit Hebden St Peter's Church. The church boasts an impressive and colourful array of hand-knitted kneelers. Turn left at the end of Church Lane and follow the track down to join a minor road. Turn right here and walk for 200m along the road to rejoin the outbound route and recross the river at the suspension bridge.

5 Head back left on the outbound path. Ignore a first path to the right and instead take the second signed path up a series of 'Postman's Steps' beside a gate after less than 100m. The steps lead up to another minor road. Here turn right and look out for the walled track – **Badger Lane** – on your left after 50m.

6 Leave the track at the first footpath on the left (signed to Burnsall). Lovely views of Wharfedale can be had from here. Follow the line of stiles to eventually emerge in **Burnsall**. Turn right to reach your start point and the bridge. You would be back in no time, but for about 11 stiles providing obstacles to slow you down at every field boundary.

Burnsall is a quintessential Dales village

− To shorten
At the suspension bridge, turn back and head up the Postman's Steps back to Burnsall. This is 1.5km shorter and saves nearly 30min.

+ To lengthen
Instead of going into Hebden, cross the suspension bridge at Waypoint 3 and follow the Dales Way footpath along the riverbank as far as you like, then retrace your steps to the bridge to continue the walk.

Burnsall Bridge

Burnsall's ancient bridge has been rebuilt and repaired due to flooding several times. Its most notable benefactor was Appletreewick-born William Craven, who was Lord Mayor of London in the early 17th century, having come to London at the age of 13 or 14 and made his fortune as a merchant tailor. Some have suggested that Craven's rags-to-riches story is the basis for the tale of Dick Whittington. Craven founded a school in Burnsall in 1601, in a building that is still used by local children to this day.

Artist at the path junction before entering Trollers Gill

WALK 7
Trollers Gill

Start/finish	Bridge just before Parcevall Hall Gardens, Skyreholme
Locate	///saying.rolled.whips
Cafes/pubs	Seasonal cafe at Parcevall Hall
Transport	DalesBus from Ilkley and Grassington to the Skyreholme turn-off near Appletreewick (1km from start)
Parking	Considerate on-road parking on approach to Parcevall Hall, with a couple of further spots in Skyreholme. Large car park at Parcevall Hall, if you pay to visit the gardens (BD23 6DE)
Toilets	No public toilets on route

Time 1½hr
Distance 3.5km (2¼ miles)
Climb 120m

A famous, although usually quiet, secluded limestone gorge that never fails to delight

The high-sided and normally dry gorge of Trollers Gill has attracted ramblers looking for a short, easily accessed but nonetheless impressively wild outing for at least 200 years. Embedded fossils, looming undercut limestone overhangs and a stream that is swallowed by subterranean vaults give Trollers Gill a bewitching quality. The sleepy meadows and open moorland that surround the gorge offer a pleasant contrast.

Crossing the bridge at the top of Trollers Gill

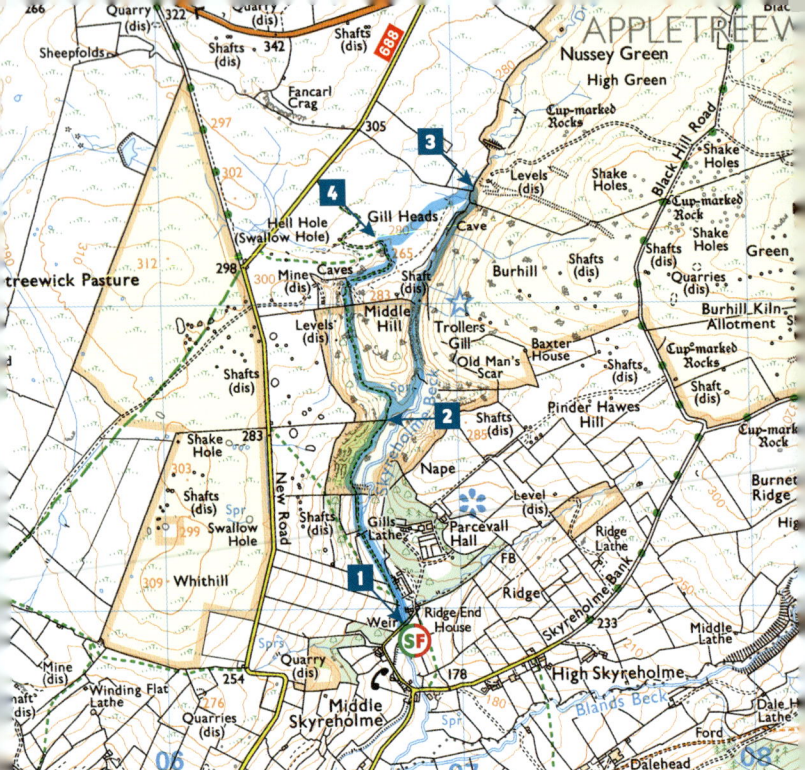

1 From the bridge just before the Parcevall Hall estate outbuildings and cafe, head back towards Skyreholme for 20m and turn right over a stile, signed Trollers Gill. Follow the pleasant path through fields, heading upstream and parallel with **Skyreholme Beck**. After 800m a short rise leads to a stile.

2 Cross the stile, gaining a view of the opening of the gorge. In 40m, take the right fork in the path (the left fork is the descent route) and follow the usually dry stream bed into **Trollers Gill**. Follow the rocky path between the encroaching walls of the gill for 700m to reach a stile at a more open area. The name 'Trollers Gill' appears to derive from an old legend that tells of trolls throwing stones down upon unwitting gorge trespassers!

3 Roughly 40m after the stile turn left over a bridge. Saplings have been planted here along a

In the rocky gorge of Trollers Gill

Yorkshire-Dales-badged path that leads upwards to escape the gill. A grassy path now continues easily over the hill to intersect a wide track.

4 Turn left along the track and follow it downhill, past a mine opening, to regain the outbound route, which is followed back to the start.

Approaching the mines on the descent route, with Simon's Seat beyond

Lead mining has left its mark on the surroundings. A mine opening and the rusty remnants of its infrastructure are seen on the descent. The roof of the mine is unstable and friable so do not be tempted to enter.

(i) *Because of the friable nature of limestone, Trollers Gill is host to a number of bolted sport climbing routes. It is not uncommon to find climbers testing their mettle on its walls.*

Trollers Gill

'The Barguest', a folkloric dog immortalised by the 1830 ballad 'The Legend of the Trollers Gill', is said to frequent the gill. There is a possibility it inspired Sir Arthur Conan Doyle's classic Sherlock Holmes novella, **The Hound of the Baskervilles**. Apparently, the Barguest turns you to stone with its Medusa-like eyes – you have been warned…!

Trollers Gill was formed in tropical seas 330–360 million years ago from shells and the harder parts of sea creatures up to 30cm long. The Carboniferous limestone of the gill has long attracted geologists, fossil-hunters and myth-makers. Caves and potholes abound: Hell Hole Cave just off route is 55m deep with over 200m of passages.

Descending the limestone defile of Trollers Gill

WALK 8
Grimwith Reservoir

Start/finish	*Grimwith Reservoir car park*
Locate	*///viewer.lashed.latches*
Cafes/pubs	*None on route*
Transport	*DalesBus 822 from Grassington to reservoir (summer Sundays only), otherwise bus to bottom of access road (about 1km from start)*
Parking	*At time of writing, free parking at reservoir (BD23 5ED)*
Toilets	*In car park*

Time 2hr
Distance 7km (4¼ miles)
Climb 100m

A simple circuit of the area's finest reservoir

Don't let the tremendously off-putting name of 'Grimwith' dissuade you – this alluring and tranquil spot is anything but grim (although the weather might sometimes be). Reservoir walks can sometimes be uninspiring, but the lofty, windswept moorland surroundings of Grimwith and the lack of roads in sight give the place a sense of remoteness. The wide grassy path across the dam is a highlight. This walk is a superb year-round outing and great for nature spotting – take your binoculars.

Crossing Grimwith's grassy dam

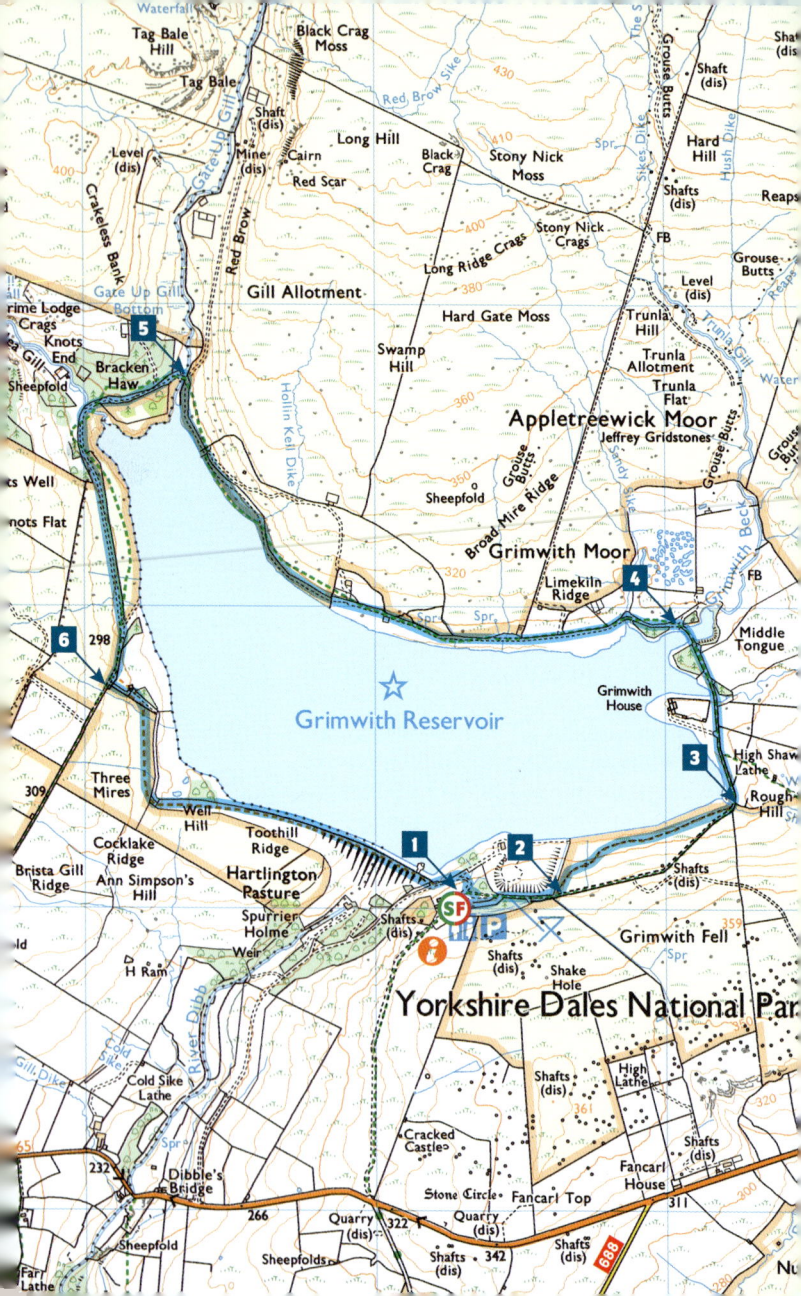

WALK 8 – GRIMWITH RESERVOIR

1 Facing the reservoir, walk right along the car park to pick up a signed track leading gradually uphill at first. This is to avoid the property of the Yorkshire Dales Sailing Club.

2 Take the signed permissive path left from the top of the rise, descending to the shore with views of the sailing club. Note that dogs must remain on leads due to the special nature and conservation areas around the shores. Just after crossing a small stream inlet, you will reach High Laithe cruck barn, a restored 400-year-old heather-thatched building.

3 Here, the path becomes a stony track and continues to reach the stone building of **Grimwith House** – now a holiday let – on the shoreline in 300m. Continue to cross a footbridge in 100m with a mini-reservoir formed by Grimwith Beck on your right.

4 After the footbridge, pass a small wood. The path then continues near the open shoreline for a further 2km around the north side of the reservoir.

5 As you reach the narrower head of the reservoir, cross another footbridge at a pleasant spot with views up **Gate Up Gill**, named after a hamlet which was flooded in order to build the reservoir. Shortly afterwards a second footbridge is crossed. Continue for 1km then look out for a signed split in the path.

High Laithe cruck barn

Above the sailing club at Grimwith with Appletreewick Moor beyond

Grimwith House at the reservoir's eastern end

6 Take the left-hand route, downhill initially, to reach and cross the huge grassy dam wall. Just past the water tower at the dam's end, turn left on the tarmac track leading back up to the car park.

> ⓘ *Red kites were once extinct in England, but a successful reintroduction programme based at nearby Harewood House has meant that these majestic birds are now a common sight in the skies across this area.*

The waters of Grimwith

Grimwith holds the largest volume of water of any reservoir in Yorkshire. It was originally built in 1864 to power the burgeoning mills of industrial Bradford, causing the hamlets of Grimwith and Gate Up to disappear forever underwater. A few outlying ruins of these dwellings can be seen on the north shore. The reservoir is a popular stop-off point for migrating birds and, depending on the time of year you visit, you might see Canada geese, widgeon, plover, curlew and many more.

Scale Haw Force near the start of the walk

WALK 9
Grassington lead mines from Hebden

Start/finish	*Hebden village centre*
Locate	*///thumb.overlooks.tightrope*
Cafes/pubs	*Cafe and pub in Hebden*
Transport	*DalesBus from Grassington*
Parking	*On-street parking in Hebden (BD23 5DX)*
Toilets	*None on route*

Time 2½hr
Distance 8km (5 miles)
Climb 260m

Follow the peaceful Hebden Beck to discover the lead mining heritage of Grassington Moor

This route follows the delightful Hebden Ghyll gradually up onto the moors to reach the fascinating remains of Grassington lead mines. Several information boards here help you make sense of the history of the landscape, which feels far more remote than it actually is. The striking chimney, flue and ruins make this a place that fires the imagination and captures the essence of a harsher bygone way of life.

Descending the winding Hebden Ghyll

WALK 9 – GRASSINGTON LEAD MINES FROM HEBDEN

1 Take High Green – on the opposite side of the B6265 from the main part of the village. Walk out of the village on this dead-end road for 500m to the reach a footpath sign leading down through a field to a waterfall at Scale Haw Force. A 50m detour can be made to see the falls, then continue along the road for a further 100m to the hamlet of **Hole Bottom**.

2 Leave the road, taking a bridleway on the right signed to Yarnbury. This good track leads over a footbridge and up alongside **Hebden Beck**. The route now follows the beck almost all the way to a dam at its head. At various points there are paths on both sides of the beck but the route never goes too far from the watercourse. You will reach the first evidence of the mining heritage of the area after 800m at a cluster of ruined buildings.

3 About 100m after the mine buildings, there are a few large stepping stones across the beck. Take these (making note of a track joining from a side valley on the right which is used on the return route) and cross the beck, continuing briefly up its left side before crossing back at a shallow ford 100m later. The beck never holds much water and can easily be crossed at many points. Continue to reach a rising gravel track after 100m.

4 Either take the track – on the beck's left side – or continue up the valley floor. Where the track veers off left, be careful to continue up the beck to cross a stile and head rightwards

Crossing Hebden Beck above the first mine ruins

Give us a hand! The long chimney flue tunnel at the mines

towards a huge conifer tree – the only one for miles around. Go gradually uphill on the path past the lonely tree, then beside a rocky tributary to reach a large cluster of ruins at **Cupola** smelt mill in 200m.

> A large information board beside a big ladder stile provides a good place to start exploring the lead mines. Make sure to visit the impressive 18m tall chimney by following a path up the line of a flue. Several tunnels can be explored with care.

Return to the Cupola mineworks and the ladder stile via the same route, or follow the slightly longer interpretive trail which leads back to the same point via a grinding mill building. The height gained affords views across Wharfedale to the Cracoe fells.

5 After exploring the lead mines, return to Hebden by retracing your route up to where it first crossed the beck at the stepping stones. Here there is an obvious side valley with mineworks at the top. Do not go up this valley but take the clear rising track which climbs the left flank of Hebden Ghyll and traverses above the outbound route. The gradient shortly eases where a gate is reached.

6 Go through the gate and continue along a grassy path. In 700m the path passes **Mossy Moor Reservoir** on its right. This is easily missed as a small embankment blocks the view. This section can be boggy after long wet periods. Continue for 400m until the path meets a track. Stray a few metres off the path to take in the hidden shoreline of Mossy Moor reservoir, which is a birdwatcher's paradise.

7 Turn sharply right – as if taking the farm track – then skirt round the right boundary of the farm to reach a signpost and gap stile in 50m. Here the path drops steeply down towards Hole Bottom. Go straight through a gate at the bottom of the steepest section, then follow the path diagonally left beside a wall down to the beck floor.

Cross a final stile and small footbridge to reach the village of **Hebden** and the start point.

> **− To shorten**
>
> Retrace your steps back to Hebden from the lead mines. This saves about 20min, though only 500m of distance.

Grassington Lead Mines

The striking chimney of the lead mines

After a first smelt mill was built at nearby Linton in 1604, lead mining began to gain momentum in the Grassington area. When the shallower surface ore was all extracted, an adit was built up Hebden Beck in order to drain deeper mineral veins. The Duke of Devonshire, whose name will be familiar to visitors to Bolton Abbey, built the Cupola smelt mill on this route in 1792. A few years later, Yarnbury Dam was built at the head of the gill. The dam provided water to power a huge wheel, which drove pumps in the mines.

To extract lead from the ore a huge furnace was needed and the long flue and chimney seen on this route were built for this. In the mid 19th century – when the mines were at their peak – the flue was 1.8km long, 170 people worked here and nearly 1000 tonnes of lead were extracted each year.

The narrowing at the lower part of Linton Falls

WALK 10
Grassington, Linton Falls and Linton

Start/finish	Grassington market square
Locate	///boater.trader.trombone
Cafes/pubs	Great choice in Grassington, the Fountaine pub in Linton
Transport	DalesBus from Skipton and Pateley Bridge
Parking	National Park visitor centre car park (BD23 5LB)
Toilets	In car park

This is a superb summer walk, when the River Wharfe is bubbling and enticing and the meadows are blooming with clover and buttercups. Plenty of visitors to the lively cobbled streets of Grassington make their way to the photogenic bridge over Linton Falls, but fewer venture further afield. The picture-postcard ford at the village green in Linton village makes an idyllic stop on this lovely ramble.

Time 2hr
Distance 6km (3¾ miles)
Climb 130m

Limestone channels and picturesque weirs on the Wharfe followed by meadows with perfect picnicking, paddling and pub stops

Linton village with the Fountaine almshouse, seen from the latter part of the walk

SHORT WALKS YORKSHIRE DALES

WALK 10 – GRASSINGTON, LINTON FALLS AND LINTON

1 From the bottom of Grassington's cobbled main street, turn left on Hebden Road, shortly passing the Yorkshire Dales National Park visitor centre. Immediately after the car park, take a signed footpath down **Sedber Lane**. This quickly becomes a delightful narrow walled path which descends to the bridge at **Linton Falls**.

> Upstream are two weirs and some popular bathing spots. Downstream the Wharfe tumbles through the 'falls' of a limestone channel.

2 Cross the river and follow the path right and right again across a tiny stone bridge to join a riverside path with the **River Wharfe** on your right. At a pebble beach by the weir, the path goes through a small gate into a wood and reaches a minor road.

3 Turn left and follow the road for 100m to a little school. Take a bridleway right immediately after this, crossing a disused railway 500m later with views of the Cracoe fells and Simon's Seat. Continue to reach a road.

4 Cross the road and take the footpath signed to Linton. Follow the path through meadows and under an old railway bridge, before becoming a wide gravel track leading into **Linton** village.

5 Go right to reach the village green. Cross the small stone bridge by the

Linton Falls and weir

ford in front of the pub and then turn right up the lane for 50m, taking a footpath along the left side of a farmhouse signed to Threapland and the B6160. The path crosses through a wall after 50m. Here head straight forward at a first signpost. **There are lots of paths in this area so take care.**

6 At a second signpost only 20m later, turn left over a stile (signed to the B6160). Stay on the high ground and then cross a stone stile keeping on the right side of a small wood. After a second stone stile, go straight across the next field past a lonely barn to a ladder stile then another stone stile. Turn sharply left here to meet the road in 20m.

7 Take the footpath opposite signed to Linton Falls. Head diagonally left across the field and through a squeeze stile to gain an escarpment above the Wharfe where, after passing a small wood, views of the river and Linton church dramatically appear.

Linton's St Michael and All Angels churchyard features the base of an Anglo-Saxon 7th-century cross. The churchyard is also reputedly haunted by the ghost of a monk from a nearby abbey.

8 The stepping stones and pebble beach on the bend of the river can be reached from here if desired on a path leading down from the escarpment. **Be warned – the stepping stones are fairly challenging to cross in all but drought conditions.** Instead, keep on the high ground then stay right of a barn and reach some houses on the

The Wharfe south of Grassington on the return route

Risking the stepping stones by St Michael and All Angels Church

dead-end road to Linton church (turn right to visit it). Turn left here for 200m to reach Linton Falls and retrace your steps back into **Grassington**.

> ### ✚ To lengthen
> Negotiating the stepping stones from Waypoint 8 and walking back to Grassington along the Dales Way path on the opposite side of the river to Linton church adds 500m of distance – an extra 10min. Turning left before retracing the ascent up the narrow, walled path and Sedber Lane to Grassington allows you to follow the Dales Way to Grassington Bridge and into the village. This adds 1km (15min).

Linton

The small hydroelectric power station at the weir above Linton Falls was first built in 1909, featuring two Archimedes screw turbines. It fell into disuse but has now been restored to a similar design and currently provides electricity to the people of Grassington. The impressive large building on Linton village green is the Fountaine Hospital Almshouse. It was commissioned by local philanthropist Richard Fountaine, who died in 1722. Supposedly to the disgruntlement of his family, Fountaine bequeathed a fund to enable locals in need to live in the almshouse: it is still home to some elderly residents.

Mixed broadleaf woodland in Grass Wood

WALK 11
Grassington Grass Wood and Ghaistrill's Strid

Time 2½hr
Distance 7km (4¼ miles)
Climb 190m

A popular scenic village, tranquil wood and meandering river with a photogenic limestone narrowing

Start/finish	Grassington market square
Locate	///boater.trader.trombone
Cafes/pubs	Great choice in Grassington
Transport	DalesBus from Skipton and Ilkley
Parking	National Park car park (BD23 5LB)
Toilets	In car park

A varied amble taking in the historic market village of Grassington, picturesque limestone-walled pasture, peaceful mixed woodland and a scenic section of the River Wharfe that includes the impressive narrowing of Ghaistrill's Strid. This enticing walk offers good nature spotting: ever-present but once-endangered red kites swooping overhead; roe deer and great speckled woodpeckers inhabiting the woods; or, on the river section, kingfishers in summer and often-shy otters feasting on trout, crayfish and barbel.

Approaching Grass Wood on the Dales Way

WALK 11 – GRASSINGTON GRASS WOOD AND GHAISTRILL'S STRID

1 Walk uphill on Main Street – the left of the two roads ascending from the market square. After 100m, follow the Dales Way sign and turn left on Chapel Street. Continue for 200m then turn right on the Dales Way up Bank Lane.

2 Bank Lane soon becomes an unpaved farm track. After 250m turn left to leave the track and continue across a field to a stile. Now part company with the Dales Way and instead head left downhill for 30m to a gate. Cross over a well-used farm track, through a gate and into another field. Continue trending downhill on a grassy path. Exit the field and bear right – effectively straight on – along a farm track for 100m. Take the right hand of two gates, cross two fields and enter **Grass Wood**.

> A Bronze Age burial mound and a ruined Brigantian settlement (Fort Gregory) are located just off route in Grass Wood. Although both can be located, there is little to see.

3 At the nature board, head straight on uphill. A sign is soon passed denoting a Bronze Age burial mound just off route. Ignore a turning signed to 'Far Gregory Fort', and roughly 50m further on the main path becomes a more pronounced track. This could be taken to slightly shorten the walk.

4 Leave the track, following the clearly signed public footpath trending right. This curves westwards through the woods, eventually descending to a nature board near a gate that accesses a road.

5 From the nature board, head left – effectively parallel with the road – on a clear path through the woods. After 500m take a path branching off right for 40m to reach a gate onto a minor road. Double back along the road for 80m, then go left through the wall before choosing the middle one of three paths. The riverbank is soon reached.

6 Continue to follow the path downstream which, but for a brief climb into the woods allowing superb views, remains on the riverbank and 1.2km later takes in the magnificent **Ghaistrill's Strid** on route to Grassington.

> The name Ghaistrill probably means 'ghost stream' and this part of the river is supposedly haunted. One spectre is said to be that of the 18th-century murderer of a Grassington doctor; he was caught and hanged, then his remains purportedly thrown in the water.

Roughly 100m before reaching the arches of the Grade 2 listed

A heron surveys the waters of Ghaistrill's Strid

The grassy banks of the Wharfe just upstream of Ghaistrill's Strid

Grassington Bridge, a pronounced path goes off to the left away from the riverbank.

> ⓘ *The name of the River Wharfe comes from an Old Norse word 'hverfi', meaning winding or bending.*

7 Follow the path up to a gate in the corner of the field just above the bridge. From the gate, ignore the first footpath on the left and instead go rightwards uphill for 20m past benches to locate a second footpath which trends left uphill. This soon straightens to pass between houses and meet Raines Lane. Cross over and continue between more houses to reach Wharfe Lane, which is followed to a crossroads. Turn right on Wood Lane to reach the main B6265 road bend in the centre of **Grassington** and the market square to the left (or, better, take an unsigned sneaky snicket on the left 50m before the main road, which leads to the market square).

> ⓘ *The picturesque early medieval settlement of Grassington has served as a location for various films and television programmes, most recently Channel 5's adaptation of All Creatures Great and Small.*

Coniston Pie above Conistone Dib

WALK 12
Conistone Dib and Pie

Start/finish	*Conistone Bridge*
Locate	*///detail.uptown.barbarian*
Cafes/pubs	*Pub and cafe in Kilnsey 200m from start*
Transport	*DalesBus from Skipton*
Parking	*On roadside before the bridge, no parking in village centre*
Toilets	*No public toilets on route*

Conistone Dib is a fine outing with a short gorge that makes a lasting impression. The scenery is tremendous, even the proximity of a small TV mast does little to mar the experience. With an array of easily visited limestone clints and grykes and the bewitching panoramic mini-summit of Conistone Pie added to the round, this is Yorkshire's landscape at its best. The gorge itself has some simple short scrambly steps, which should not put anyone off.

Time 1½hr
Distance 4.5km (2¾ miles)
Climb 165m

A delightful limestone gorge leads to a spectacular high-plateau with a distinctive pie-shaped sub-summit

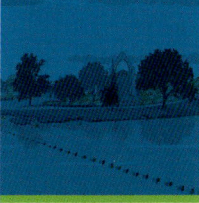

The dry valley of Conistone Dib

SHORT WALKS YORKSHIRE DALES

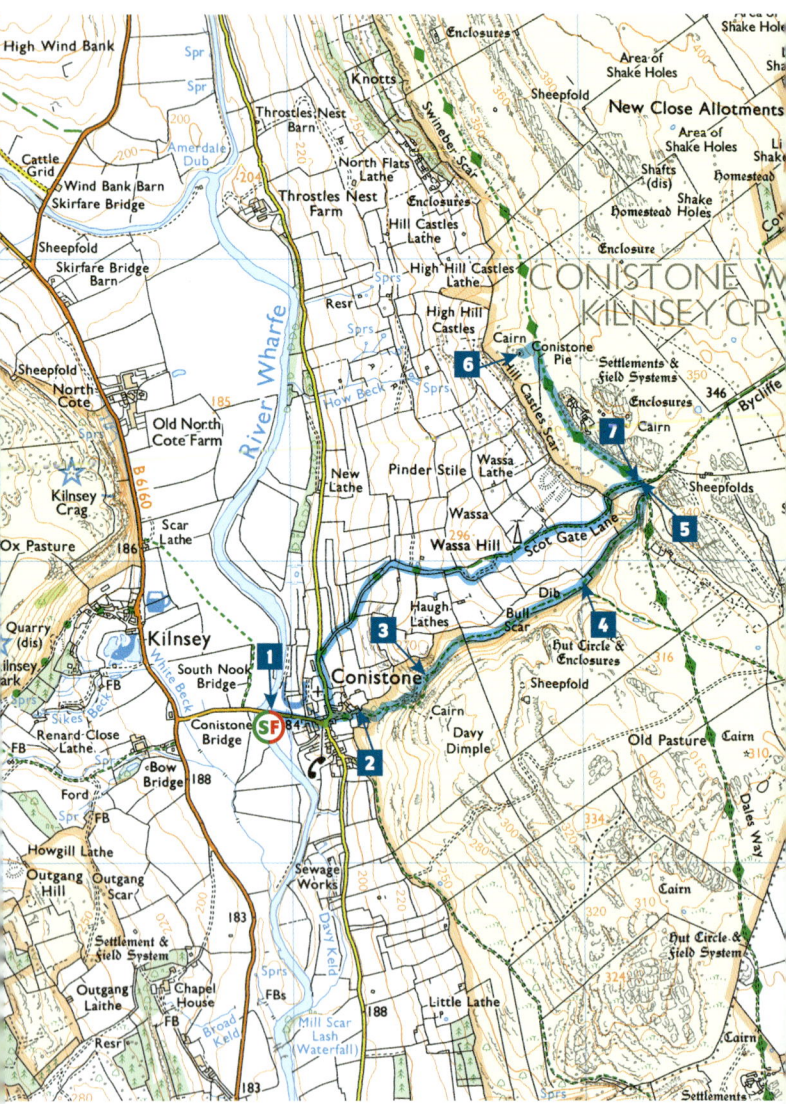

WALK 12 – CONISTONE DIB AND PIE

1 From the bridge head up the road into the village. Bear left at the triangular roundabout and take an unsurfaced track on the right 20m afterwards. Staying right (straight on) the track leads, in 100m, to a gate.

2 A short grassy section beyond the gate quickly gives way to an easily negotiated section of stepped limestone up a small, long-absent waterfall. Once over this, the walls narrow – to a couple of metres wide in places – and the gorge of **Conistone Dib** provides a sense of seclusion. The dry bed is well travelled and will pose no significant difficulty. The various features of the gorge include a water-worn slab with a boot-wide channel.

3 On emerging from the narrow part of the gorge, the valley broadens to provide a long and level grassy clearing. Head eastward through the clearing, watched over by the limestone crag of **Bull Scar** above on the right. Just beyond Bull Scar a path escapes to the right (south) at a junction.

While 'dib' can mean a small hollow or dip, a 'dib' is an archaic term for a pool (in Scotland 'dib' is still occasionally used to denote a puddle). Most likely 'Conistone Dib' once boasted a pool, probably at the foot of the initial dry waterfall.

The dry waterfall at the bottom of Conistone Dib

Negotiating the boot-wide channel of Conistone Dib

4 From the path junction, continue through the hanging valley to its craggy conclusion. A relatively steep but easy ascent over short passages of stepped limestone exits the small hanging valley. Go right at the top then almost immediately switch back left to reach a gate with a four-way signpost.

5 The route now follows the Dales Way: this is almost straight ahead on a wide grassy path, crossing over a farm track after 20m. The distinctive round 'wart' of the grassy plateau, **Conistone Pie**, is reached in 500m.

This section of the 80-mile Dales Way route runs along the top of the evocatively named Hill Castles Scar. Conistone Pie gives Yorkshire-Tea-box views west to the impressive overhanging Kilnsey Crag and north towards Kettlewell.

6 From Conistone Pie retrace the Dales Way path to reach the farm track. It is worth deviating left uphill for 40m or so at any one of several amenable spots to take in the impressive and photogenic limestone paving above the path.

> ⓘ *The Yorkshire Dales are generally named after their rivers: Wharfedale with its River Wharfe is one example.*

7 Turn right along the farm track and continue without complication back down to the edge of **Conistone**, where a left turn on the minor road delivers you to the triangular roundabout in the village. Turn right to reach your start point.

> ⓘ *The majority of sheep seen in these parts are Swaledales. These hardy hill creatures are so prevalent that they are an emblem of the Yorkshire Dales National Park.*

Mossdale

High on Conistone Moor, above the limestone paving, lies the lonely valley of Mossdale. Here Mossdale Beck disappears underground into a severely dangerous cave system prone to flooding. On 24 June 1967, 10 cavers left behind a settled summer's day to enter the dark subterranean network; six would never return. Four cavers left early to go back to the valley. However, with deteriorating weather one of the four, Morag Forbes, retraced her steps and to her horror discovered Mossdale Beck had flooded the cave. The alarm was sounded, yet despite herculean efforts by local cavers, volunteers and emergency services (including an attempted diverting of the beck), six young cavers perished. It is a solemn space: the six bodies remain deep within the caves. Plaques at the cave and a cairn commemorate the tragedy.

Descending the track back to Conistone

The towering limestone walls of Malham Cove

WALK 13
Malham Cove, Gordale Scar and Janet's Foss

Start/finish	*Malham village centre*
Locate	*///stage.sardine.patching*
Cafes/pubs	*Good choice in Malham, seasonal refreshments at Gordale Bridge*
Transport	*DalesBus from Skipton*
Parking	*National Park car park (BD23 4DA)*
Toilets	*In village centre*

Time 2½hr
Distance 8km (5 miles)
Climb 200m

A circuit visiting some of the finest natural limestone formations in the country – a walk not to be missed

This is without a doubt one of the most splendid walks in Yorkshire. The towering cliffs of Malham Cove have drawn visitors to the area since the 18th century. The otherworldly limestone paving above the cove and the spectacular gorge of Gordale Scar are highlights of this popular circuit. The wooded pool of Janet's Foss and the ancient meadows on route add to this irresistible outing. There are approximately 400 stone steps to the cove's top – the only strenuous part of the walk.

Approaching the giant cleft of Gordale Scar

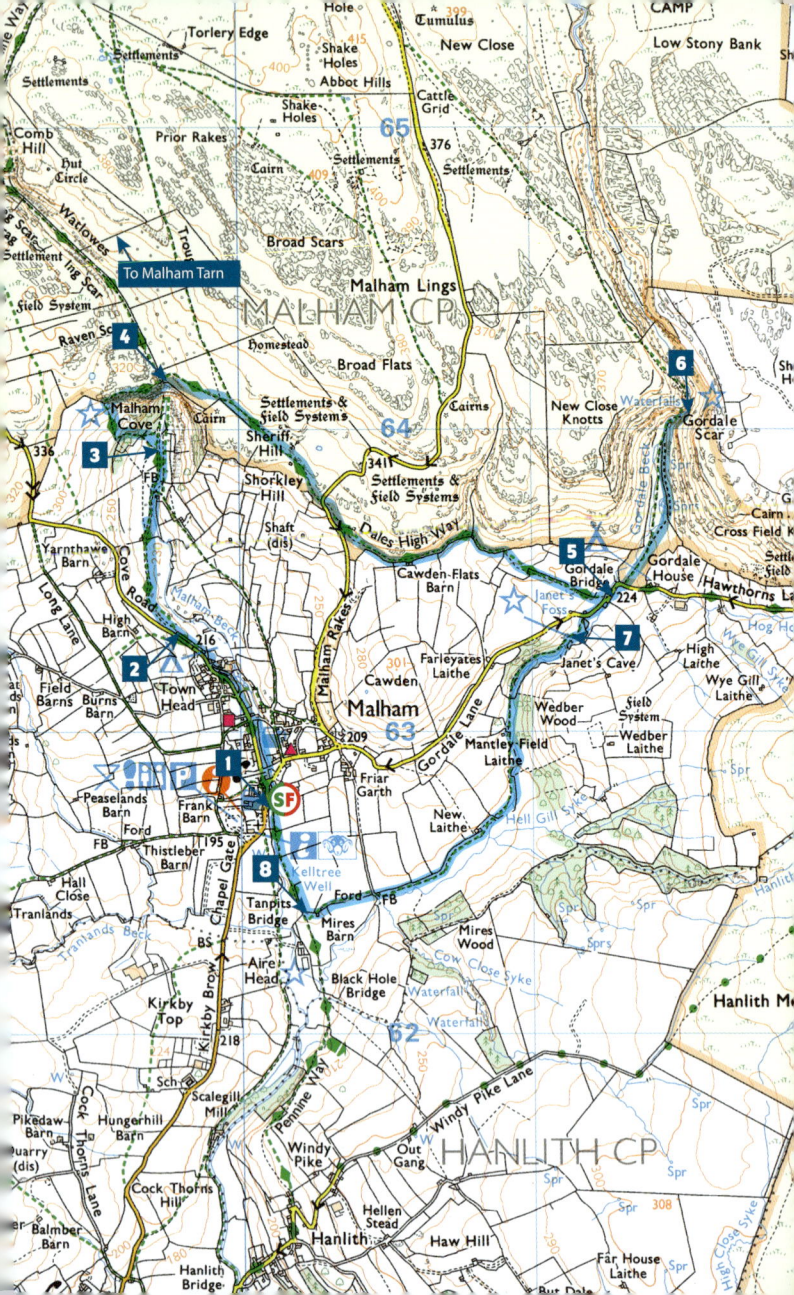

WALK 13 – MALHAM COVE, GORDALE SCAR AND JANET'S FOSS

1 Walk through the village centre to the bridge near the Buck Inn. Here there is a sign pointing straight ahead to Malham Cove. Follow the road initially; opposite the village hall take the woodland walk path on the right to avoid most of this section of road. After 200m a view of the cove opens up ahead.

2 Here take a large and obvious signed path right to Malham Cove. The path affords views of the breathtaking face of rock before dropping towards the foot of the cliffs beside **Malham Beck**.

3 The path forks near the foot of **Malham Cove**. Make a detour straight ahead to get a close-up view of the phenomenal wall of limestone. Then go left, steeply ascending a series of stone steps up the side of the cove and turn right at the top to cross the huge expanse of limestone paving on top of the cove. The clints (slabs) and grykes (fissures) of the cove's limestone paving are uneven underfoot and require care. At the far side of the paving, the path crosses a wall.

> Malham Cove is a natural wonder – an 80m-high sheer curving cliff formed by a waterfall of glacial meltwater after the last Ice Age. The spectacular limestone paving at its top was also formed by retreating glaciers; it is one of the best examples of its kind in the world.

The huge stretch of limestone paving on top of the cove

SHORT WALKS YORKSHIRE DALES

4 Head right here signed to Gordale. Follow the wide grassy path, crossing a minor road after 500m and heading in the same direction. The path stays beside a wall for another 500m before crossing the wall at a well-signed point and dropping down to **Gordale Bridge**, where there is often a large refreshments van.

5 To visit the magnificent **Gordale Scar** turn left up the road for 50m and take the signed path left through a campsite to reach the huge limestone cleft in 600m.

Gordale Scar has inspired famous poets and artists over the years, including William Wordsworth and JMW Turner. James Ward's famous painting of Gordale is exhibited in the Tate gallery in London.

6 Retrace your steps to the bridge. A right turn on the road at Gordale leads to a path left signed to Malham. Take this, reaching the waterfalls and enticing pool of **Janet's Foss** almost immediately. Janet's Foss was formerly used for sheep dipping. Janet probably refers to a fairy queen believed to live in a cave behind the fall.

7 Continue on the path, following the wooded limestone defile of **Gordale Beck** downstream. This eventually opens into meadowland and a barn is passed on the outskirts of **Malham**.

Continuing to Gordale from high above Malham Cove

WALK 13 – MALHAM COVE, GORDALE SCAR AND JANET'S FOSS

8 Continue on the main path rightwards to reach the village, crossing a stone footbridge over the beck to the start point.

✚ To lengthen
A fairly tough but worthwhile extension can be made to visit the windswept Malham Tarn, high up on the limestone plateau. After crossing the paving above the cove, turn left up the impressive Watlowes valley on the well-signed Pennine Way to eventually reach the shores of Malham Tarn in 2km, Return the same way to rejoin the main route. Allow 2hr extra.

▬ To shorten
Missing out the visit to Gordale Scar cuts over 1km off the distance, saving 30min.

Janet's Foss

Sailor on Embsay Reservoir beneath Embsay Crag

WALK 14
Embsay Crag and Reservoir

Start/finish	Car park near Elm Tree Inn, Embsay village centre
Locate	///simmer.deflation.booth
Cafes/pubs	Pub and cafe in Embsay
Transport	DalesBus from Skipton
Parking	Embsay village car park on Main Street (BD23 6RE)
Toilets	At the steam railway station (400m off route)

Time 2hr
Distance 5.5km (3½ miles)
Climb 230m

An attractive reservoir and craggy mini-summit on the expansive Embsay Moor

Encompassing a village, sleepy fields, a boating reservoir and a splendid ascent on well-trodden bracken-lined paths to the panoramic gritstone of Embsay Crag, this is a pleasing circuit that ventures into the looming moorland wildness just beyond Skipton, the southern gateway to the Yorkshire Dales. Note that dogs are not permitted on Embsay Crag and Barden Moor.

The Embsay Crag path above the reservoir

1 Exit the back of the car park into the pasture and head left, trending up to the top corner of the field where two paths converge. Pass over a stile into the next field and continue along the well-signed path through fields just above the village school. Embsay Crag looms majestically above on the right. Cross over a track and enter the next field, continuing easily across two fields to emerge at the usually quiet narrow road.

2 Turn right and follow the road up to the car park at **Embsay Reservoir** and continue through it to the boathouse.

3 Head right along the track towards Embsay Moor, but 50m after the

WALK 14 – EMBSAY CRAG AND RESERVOIR

boathouse slip through a gate to take a permissive path beside the reservoir. Although this looks like it can be followed most of the way round the water to join the main route up Embsay Crag, it does not connect, so leave the permissive path at the northwestern corner of the reservoir and take a grassy left branch for 100m to return to the approach track.

4 Turn right onto the track, before immediately taking a well-signed right turn along a path on the moor side of the walled reservoir, heading directly towards Embsay Crag. At a fork in the path, trend right next to the reservoir wall. Cross a bridge before climbing on a broad sandy path away from the reservoir and directly uphill towards the obvious summit to reach a junction of paths.

5 Ignore the steep direct approach to the summit and instead take the path that branches left and gives a more gradual ascent. This eventually loops pleasantly back towards the summit of **Embsay Crag**. The fell top affords superb views south down Airedale and west towards Pendle Hill in Lancashire.

6 From the summit, follow the clear path eastwards steadily downhill for 400m where it arcs right to leave the moor via a gate.

7 The descending path soon becomes a walled track leading to a

Views of Airedale and Pendle Hill from Embsay Crag

87

SHORT WALKS YORKSHIRE DALES

Golden-ringed dragonfly at Embsay Reservoir

right onto a signed footpath. Now follow this through two fields to reach the field above the car park in **Embsay**.

Embsay originated as a Saxon-era village, which witnessed a Viking raid in AD874, boasts a pub, a shop and a relaxed, sleepy air. Embsay was the birthplace of 1970s rock-climbing legend Ron Fawcett.

farm. Thereafter it is surfaced and leads uncomplicatedly to a T-junction with the Barden–Embsay road.

8 Turn right and follow the road until just past the churchyard, then turn

> ⓘ *In summer you may notice small green bushes of tiny black bilberries covering the moorland. These are edible and supposedly help you see in the dark.*

– To shorten
Leave out the fell ascent and simply make a circuit of the reservoir on obvious paths then return to the village via the outbound route. This gives a walk of just over 3km (1hr).

Heading towards the excellent mini summit of Embsay Crag

WALK 15
Skipton Woods and Castle

Start/finish	*Skipton Castle*
Locate	*///mountains.hooks.myth*
Cafes/pubs	*Great choice in Skipton*
Transport	*Regular trains from Leeds, Bradford and Lancaster*
Parking	*On Skipton marketplace or High Street car park*
Toilets	*In High Street car park (BD23 1ED)*

An attractive walk of surprising magnificence – with a circuit this good on the doorstep it is little surprise that Skipton routinely features in 'happiest places to live in Great Britain' lists. Encompassing the soaring ramparts of Skipton Castle, fascinating Georgian canal systems and the site of a Civil War battery, to exchange the bustling 'Gateway to the Dales' town for this peaceful walk is to embrace a historical tour in a truly uplifting setting.

Time 1½hr
Distance 3.5km (2¼ miles)
Climb 85m

An impressive patchwork of woodland, waterways and panoramic pasture, seamed with a thousand years of English history

Skipton's Georgian canal and Holy Trinity Church

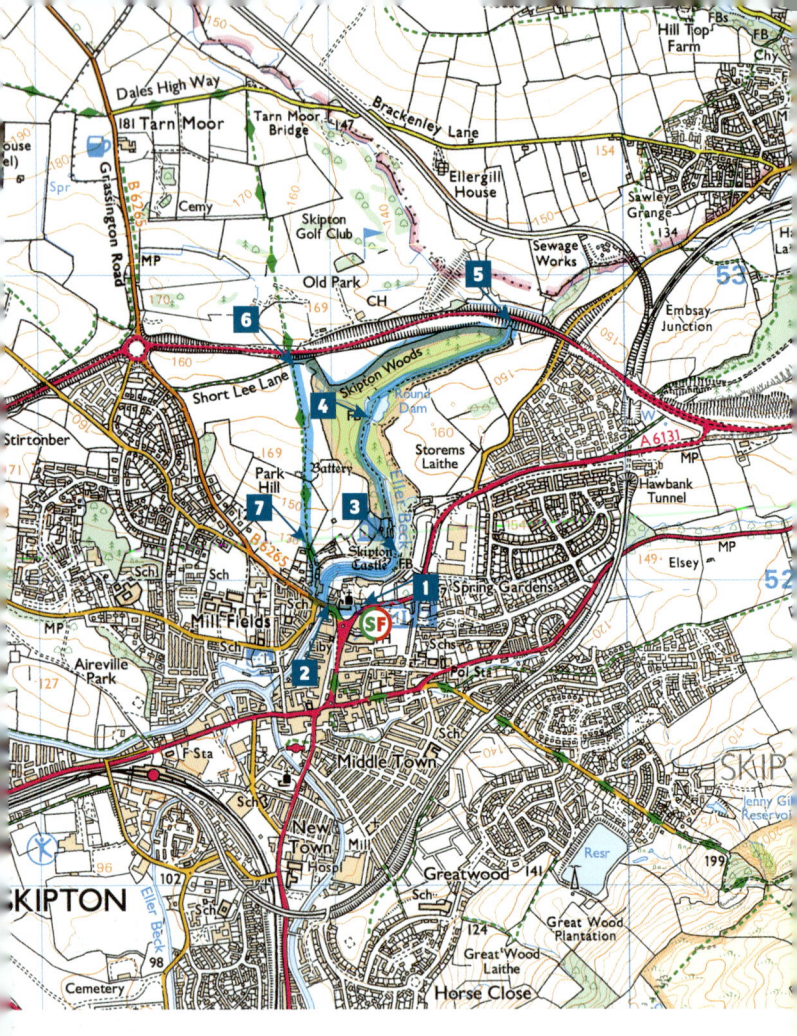

1 From the former portcullis front gate of Skipton Castle, enter the churchyard and follow the path running the length of the medieval Holy Trinity Church to exit via a stone arch.

2 Turn right, passing the Castle Inn and cross a bridge, where an immediate right turn down steps leads to the canal. The Georgian Leeds–Liverpool canal, finally completed in 1816, is

WALK 15 – SKIPTON WOODS AND CASTLE

one of the most impressive feats of British transportation infrastructure ever built. Head away from the town. The path has to its right a Georgian canal spur that has incorporated the former castle moat and, to its left, Eller Beck; the raised gangway between the two waterways is delightful.

> This canal here is actually the Springs Branch Line – a spur from the main canal built at the behest of Lord Thanet in the 1770s to serve his limestone quarries. The remnants of tramlines connecting the canal with the quarries can still be seen today.

3 Cross **Eller Beck** via a slender bridge to emerge on a minor dead-end road near a former Georgian sawmill. Turn right and continue through a gate into the woods. Take the broad, well-surfaced path swinging up a short rise to pass The Huntress – an ethereal willow sculpture. Continue without complication to reach a bridge crossing to the right over Eller Beck, near an impressive carved stone information board and timeline near Round Dam at the confluence of Sougha Gill and Eller Beck.

4 Follow the broad path with the large pond of **Round Dam** on the right and the becalmed Eller Beck on the left. After 500m a wooden bridge crosses the beck. Ignore this and continue on the right-hand side of Eller Beck for a further 80m or so to reach

On the raised walkway below the castle ramparts

The willow sculpture of The Huntress in autumn

On Park Hill looking back towards Embsay Crag

two tunnels that carry the beck under a main road.

5 Cross the bridge left over the tunnels and after 20m bear right to climb uphill on a good path next to the boundary of **Skipton Woods**. After 500m, pass a steep path coming up from the left and continue, eventually trending right to exit the woods via a gate onto Short Lee Lane. After only 30m, take a left over a stone-stepped stile hidden in the trees.

6 Head up **Park Hill** on a faint grassy path parallel with, and roughly 30m from, the boundary of the woods. At the top of Park Hill cross a stone stile in the wall to the right of two gates.

To the right are the earthwork remnants of a Civil War battery, although you would need a lot of imagination to picture the cannons and the siege of royalist Skipton Castle by parliamentary soldiers here in the 1640s.

Descend to the left-hand corner of the steep field to reach a gate.

7 Go through the gate and along the short lane to Chapel Hill. Follow this easily downhill to reach the main road, then turn left to join the outbound route at the canal steps.

Skipton Castle

The former portcullis front gate of Skipton Castle

Skipton Castle is a Norman-era castle that dates from 1090. The initial structure was largely earth and timber. Doing little to repel marauding Scots, this was soon superseded by the magnificent castle built from Yorkshire gritstone. The castle served as one of the last significant royalist strongholds in the north during the English Civil War. It finally fell after a protracted on-off three-year siege in 1645 – although this may have had more to do with its relative remoteness than its admittedly impressive fortifications. The site of a battery involved in the siege is passed on the walk, while the inside of the castle is well worth a visit.

USEFUL INFORMATION

Tourism bodies

Yorkshire Dales National Park www.yorkshiredales.org.uk

The National Trust www.nationaltrust.org.uk

Welcome to Yorkshire www.welcometoyorkshire.com

Tourist information centres

Ilkley www.ilkley.org

Grassington – National Park visitor centre www.yorkshiredales.org.uk/places/grassington_national_park_centre

Skipton www.skiptontownhall.co.uk

Malham – National Park visitor centre www.yorkshiredales.org.uk/places/malham_national_park_centre

Travel

DalesBus www.dalesbus.org

Northern Rail www.northernrailway.co.uk

© Rachel Crolla and Carl McKeating 2025
First edition 2025
ISBN: 978 1 78631 232 7
eISBN: 978 1 78765 158 6

Printed in Singapore by KHL printing on responsibly sourced paper.
A catalogue record for this book is available from the British Library.
All photographs are by the author unless otherwise stated.
Cover illustration of Bolton Abbey by Clare Crooke
© Crown copyright and database rights 2025 OS AC0000810376
Cicerone's EU representative for GPSR compliance is Easy Access System Europe, Mustamäe tee 50, 10621 Tallinn, Estonia. Email gpsr.requests@easproject.com.

CICERONE

Cicerone Press, Juniper House, Murley Moss, Oxenholme Road, Kendal, Cumbria, LA9 7RL

www.cicerone.co.uk

Dedication

The authors would like to dedicate this book to the memory of Frances Armstrong

Updates to this Guide

While every effort is made to ensure the accuracy of guidebooks as they go to print, changes can occur during the lifetime of an edition. Any updates that we know of for this guide will be on the Cicerone website (www.cicerone.co.uk/1232/updates), so please check before planning your trip. We also advise that you check information about transport, accommodation and shops locally. Even rights of way can be altered over time. We are always grateful for information about any discrepancies between a guidebook and the facts on the ground, sent by email to updates@cicerone.co.uk.

Register your book: To sign up to receive free updates, special offers and GPX files where available, create a Cicerone account and register your purchase via the 'My Account' tab at www.cicerone.co.uk.